T0208134

River of Stars

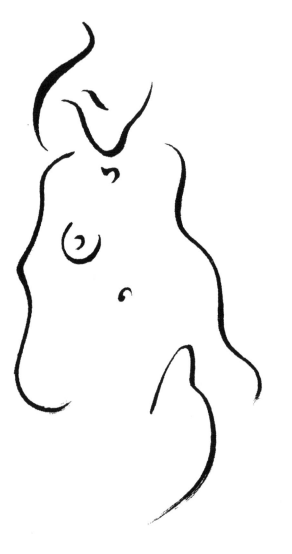

RIVER OF STARS

Selected Poems of
Yosano Akiko

Translated from the Japanese
by *Sam Hamill* and *Keiko Matsui Gibson*

Illustrated by *Stephen Addiss*

SHAMBHALA
Boston & London
1996

SHAMBHALA PUBLICATIONS, INC.
Horticultural Hall
300 Massachusetts Avenue
Boston, Massachusetts 02115
http://www.shambhala.com

A number of the poems in this book originally appeared in the
journals *Agni, Alaska Quarterly Review, Five Points, Prarie Schooner, Mosaic,*
and *Tricycle: The Buddhist Review, Bombay Gin,* and in the books *Only Companion*
and *The Erotic Spirit,* by Sam Hamill both published by
Shambhala Publications.

Distributed in the United States by Random House, Inc.,
and in Canada by Random House of Canada Ltd

LIBRARY OF CONGRESS CATALOGING-IN-PUBLICATION DATA
Yosano, Akiko, 1878–1942.
River of stars: selected poems of Yosano Akiko/translated from
the Japanese by Sam Hamill and Keiko Matsui Gibson.
p.   cm.
Includes index.
ISBN 1-57062-146-2
1. Yosano, Akiko, 1878–1942—Translations into English.
2. Waka—Translations into English.   I. Hamill, Sam.
II. Gibson, Keiko Matsui, 1953–   .   III. Title.
PL8196.O8R59   1997   96-25654
895.6′144—dc20   CIP

BVG 01

Dusk, the Omi Sea,
a lone plover skimming waves,
and with each soft cry,
my heart too, like dwarf bamboo,
stirred, longing for bygone days.

Ōmi no umi
yunami chidori
na ga nakeba
kokoro mo shinu ni
inishie omōyu

—HITOMARO, *Man'yōshū*

Contents

Introduction

Yosano Akiko was born December 7, 1878, in Sakai, Japan, one of eight children of the owner of a confectionery shop in a suburb of Osaka. When she died sixty-three years later in May 1942, she was the most famous and controversial female writer in Japan, having published seventy-five books, of which twenty volumes were original poetry including seventeen thousand tanka* and five hundred poems in free verse, as well as the definitive translation into modern Japanese of *The Tale of Genji* by Murasaki Shikibu. She has been called a princess, a queen, and a "goddess of poetry," the very embodiment of early-twentieth-century Japanese Romanticism, feminism, pacifism, and social reform. She dominates her epoch to such a degree that it is commonly referred to as the Age of Akiko.

Despite being raised in an atmosphere of strict traditional social constraints, the child Akiko quickly developed precocious literary enthusiasms and began to develop her prodigious talent as she explored her great-

---

*A poetic form of thirty-one syllables in the pattern of 5-7-5-7-7 syllabic lines.

grandparents' library. Her father loved the arts, and her great-grandfather was renowned as a "master's master" in the region because of his formidable knowledge of classical Chinese literature and his accomplished haiku. As a child, she spent three years being raised by an aunt because her father despised her at birth, believing she would be male, his feelings compounded by the accidental death of Akiko's elder brother two months earlier. Her mother was forced to sneak through the night to visit the child. Only with the birth of a third son did her father permit Akiko's return to the household. Once he witnessed her passion for learning, he provided her with the best possible education and gave her his undying admiration. He also imposed the most severe and archaic familial restraints, refusing to let her out even in daylight unless accompanied by a servant.

Graduating from an all-girl high school, she studied the first imperial Japanese poetry anthology, *Man'yōshū*, Sei Shonagon's famous *Pillow Book* describing life among the court literati, and *Genji.* Besides studying the classics of Japan, she read European literature and history and contemporary poetry of her time. And she wrote poetry. At the age of nineteen, she published her first tanka in a local journal, and within the next three years became prominent in literary circles around Osaka and Kyoto.

In 1900, a tanka poet named Tekkan, the leader of a new romantic movement, discovered her poems and began teaching her work, bringing her into his new poetry group in Tokyo. She would come to help him edit their journal, *Myōjō*, over the following seven years and again during its revival from 1921 to 1927.

Yosano Hiroshi was the son of a Buddhist priest. Disinclined toward his father's occupation, he lived in poverty and on his stepbrother's charity, taking the pen name Tekekan and dedicating himself to infusing tanka with the spirit of masculinism, attempting to make it more modern in sensibility and well as in use of language. He had married the daughter of a wealthy merchant, using the dowry to fund his literary journal, but quickly lost favor with his father-in-law, who demanded a divorce. In retreat, Tekkan visited Osaka, where he met two young close friends and admirers, Akiko and Yamakawa Tomiko, both of whom quickly fell in love with him. The three began writing poems together. Returning to Tokyo, Tekkan promised to marry Akiko as soon as his divorce was complete. She wrote him adoring letters. She threatened suicide; Tekkan's wife wrote back to dissuade her. Upon the departure of Tekkan's wife, Akiko moved to Tokyo.

Yosano Akiko's first and most famous book, *Midaregami* ("Tangled Hair"), was published two months later, and two months after that, Akiko and Tekkan were married. Not only did Tekkan remain in contact with his former wife, professing his devotion to her, but he apparently constantly begged her for money. Soon

Tekkan's former wife returned with their son to live in Tokyo.

Meanwhile Akiko's friend and Tekkan's former lover Tomiko had married and moved to Tokyo, but her husband died at twenty-three from tuberculosis. Tomiko revived her affair with Tekkan, who persuaded her to enter Japan Women's College. There she became friends with yet another of Tekkan's paramours, Masuda Masako, and together with Akiko the three published a book of poems called *Lovers' Clothes*. The poems so shocked the community that Tomiko and Masako were suspended from school.

Tekkan's work and reputation was already in decline, whereas Akiko was achieving genuine fame. She became the money-earning member of the household while Tekkan suffered *sturm und drang* and abysmal angst. In November 1911, Tekkan sailed for a three-year visit to France, to be joined six months later by Akiko. She remained in France only six months, visiting Germany, Holland, England, and Manchuria on her journey. It was the last time she was separated from her beloved Tekkan. Her European travels also inspired and reinforced her convictions regarding the oppression of women, and she struggled ceaselessly all her life against prejudice and the arrogance of the powerful, daring even to question the emperor during the Russo-Japanese War of 1904. She was the first poet in Japanese history to publicly and openly criticize the emperor, an act which so infuriated the populace that her house was stoned. She spoke against the execution of radicals in 1912 and later, in 1916, became a leading writer in the first Japanese feminist journal, *Blue Stocking.*

She was also a remarkable scholar. Together with Tekkan and a third editor, she compiled an authoritative fifty-volume set of Japanese classics, translated a modernized version of *The Tale of Genji,* and edited a new edition of the *Man'yōshū.* And during all this time, she gave birth to thirteen children, raising eleven to adulthood.

She argued on behalf of a poetry that spoke directly from the core of one's daily life in a language stripped of artifice or literary device. At the time *Midaregami* was published, tanka had degenerated into set phrases and images much like the sonnet in late Victorian England; it had become the set form for an amusing poetry in polite society. Akiko sought to return it to the best lyrical tradition, as it was found in the *Man'yōshū* and *Kokinshū,* the tenth-century tanka anthology; to write tanka rooted in direct, firsthand experience, whether subjective or objective. Her "modernism," which precedes the monumental changes in Western poetry made by Ezra Pound and T. S. Eliot only a few years later, is based on principles almost identical to the High Moderns: she developed a poetry, to paraphrase Pound, that was "harder, saner, cut closer to the bone."

Akiko advocated a poetry that requires the author to look directly into the heart to reveal the true emotional complexity found there. In a free-verse poem, "Women Are Plunder," she addresses her own weaknesses as she demands an elevated awareness on the part of women obsessed with materialism. Her deeply ambivalent yet passionate love for Tekkan, the resentment that crept into her memories, and her evolving commitment to Buddhism all contributed to a poetry rich in self-revelation but that also spoke with great clarity about the lives of men and especially woman and the psychology of erotic love. She is simultaneously highly representative of her own time and timeless in her evocation of romantic love. If she finds a degree of erotic attraction to a young monk, of if she finds sublime erotic appeal in the mysterious smile of the Buddha, it is not for the purpose of shocking the reader that she writes about it in her poems, but because the experience itself is authentic. If poems addressing her triangulated love life with Tekkan were shocking to the general public, it was only because convention had proscribed women from speaking directly of this practice that had been common for centuries. Her financial successes, and they were many, were products of work performed for economic necessity and were followed by long periods of extreme poverty.

When Yosano Akiko died in May 1942, Japan had become entangled in the worst kind of militarism, engaging in a brutal Pacific war that many Japanese then believed to be inevitable. In a bizarre interpretation of the ancient Shinto religion, Japanese pilots believed they rode kamikaze, divine winds, against a powerful America bent on invading Japan. The Japanese and American public had engaged in the most despicable racism and nationalism in media campaigns for ten years prior to the invasion of Pearl Harbor. To the Japanese, Americans were presented as aggressive hairy apes; to the Americans, Japanese were presented as yellow monkeys. National animosities had been exacerbated by almost daily agitation in the media in both countries. Akiko, ever the pacifist, must have been heartbroken. Her gift to humanity was her passionate, undying love—erotic love, spiritual love, familial love.

The pure genius, the nerve and verve, of Yosano Akiko are beyond dispute. She was as unyielding in her literary and personal commitments as in her social conscience, often a lonely voice protesting Japanese imperialism and the fate of women in a rigorously ritualized society. But her poetry guarantees her eternal flame in the annals of history.

> Was it a thousand
> years ago or only
> yesterday we parted?
> Even now, on my shoulder,
> I feel your friendly hand.

Sam Hamill and Keiko Matsui Gibson
January 1996

Tanka

Immersed in my hot
bath like a lovely lily
growing in a spring,
my twenty-year-old body—
so beautiful, so sublime.

Fresh from my hot bath,
I dressed slowly before
the tall mirror,
a smile for my own body.
Innocence so long ago!

Wet with spring rain,
my lover finally comes
to my poor house
like a woman in love
under trees of pink blossoms.

Gently, I open
the door to eternal
mystery, the flowers
of my breasts cupped,
offered with both my hands.

Following his bath,
I gave my handsome lover
my best purple robe
to protect him from the cold.
He blushed, and was beautiful.

I whisper, "Good night,"
slipping silently from his room
in the spring evening,
and pause at his kimono,
and try it on for size.

The handsome boatman,
singing, floating the river,
fills me with longing—
he's thrilled just remembering
last night's port-of-call girl.

So all alone
beside the temple bell:
I stole away
to secretly meet you here.
But now the fog has cleared.

By a nameless stream,
small and very beautiful,
last night spent alone—
these broad, desolate fields
in the harsh summer dawn.

Kiyomizu Temple's
picturesque across Gion:
cherry blossoms in
moonlight, these passing faces,
every one so beautiful!

Sutras grow bitter
on this long spring evening.
Deep within the shrine,
O twenty-five bodhisattvas,
please accept my humble song.

You've never explored
this tender flesh or known
such stormy blood.
Do you not grow lonely, friend,
forever preaching the Way?

He does not return.
Spring evening slowly descends.
Only this empty heart
and, falling over my koto,*
strands of my disheveled hair.

*A classical Japanese stringed instrument played in a sitting position.

Raindrops continue
to fall on white lotus leaves.
While my lover paints,
I open the umbrella
on his little boat.

Among the new leaves
of all these budding trees,
I see everywhere
your smiling friendly face,
O my beloved Buddha.

A man, like a twig
of the blossoming wild plum,
is sufficient:
it's temporary, and
temporary our parting.

Standing beside him
at his poor mother's grave,
we place the anise sprig
upon her tomb. And I weep
the tears of a common-law wife.

With teary eyes, she
turns to me for sympathy,
but all I can see
reflected on the water
is a lonely harvest moon.

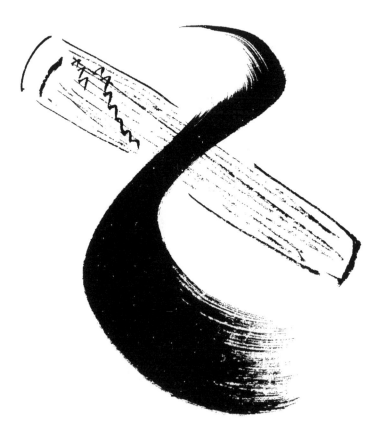

A long, restless night,
now my tangled hair
sweeps the strings of my koto.
Three months into spring
and I've not played one note.

Hearing your poem,
I had to bite my sleeve
to keep from crying
out in the Osaka inn
that bitter cold autumn day.

And now you must ask
whether I've written new songs.
I am the mythic
koto with twenty-five strings,
but without a bridge for sound.

The gods wish it so:
a life ends with a shatter—
with my great broadax
I demolish my koto.
Oh, listen to that sound!

Like a summer flower,
fragile as its slender stem,
love wastes me away.
Yet I shall blossom, crimson
under the bright noonday sun.

From her shoulder,
falling over the sutra,
a strand of unruly hair.
A lovely girl and a monk.
The burden of early spring.

Does the pale priest see,
just after sunset, the girl
who dreams beneath
a flowering pink tree
this beautiful spring evening?

One note from the flute
and the priest's hand hesitates
above the sutra.
He furrows his dark brow.
He's still not quite mature.

While mother begins
chanting a deathbed sutra,
beside her, the
tiny feet of her infant,
oh so beautiful to see.

After hearing my
heartfelt song, he disappeared
in a veil of tears.
Now ten dark days have passed
without a sign of return.

Don't complain to me,
don't hesitate, just hurry
to meet those soft hands
that are patiently waiting
to help you out of your clothes.

Not so long ago,
I was jealous of her beauty.
And now the incense
burns, smoke curling through the hair
of my friend whom we shall bury.

In bright spring sunshine
adoring lovers recline
against a white wall.
A lonely stranger watches.
Dusk enters the wisteria.

Hitting my koto,
a single plum fell
at noontime at our house
while you were beside the clear
river reciting poetry.

His hand on my neck,
he whispers softly of love.
Dawn. Wisteria.
No way I can detain him,
my one-night-only lover!

Early summer comes
to this ancient mountain
temple where, for his
wake, I carefully arrange
a bouquet of white flowers.

Did you really think
I could recite the sutras
free of all anguish?
The least teachings of Buddha?
The best teachings of Buddha?

I say his poem,
propped against this frozen wall,
in the late evening,
as bitter autumn rain
continues to fall.

A handsome oarsman
and an impeccable young
priest aboard—oh, how
I despise this bright moonlight
on our lotus-viewing boat.

Voice still immature,
the young monk recites sutras,
his face half revealed
in moonlight as my brother
rows the lotus-viewing boat.

Testing, tempting me
forever, those youthful lips
barely touching the
frosty cold drops of dew
on a white lotus blossom.

Mistaken again!
I thought, for just a moment,
I saw my lover's face—
but mischievous, capricious,
all the little gods of love.

Hair in morning tangles,
perhaps I should comb it out
with spring rainwater
as it drips from the ink-black
feathers of swallows' wings.

Where gentle spring winds
scatter pale cherry blossoms
near the pagoda,
on the wings of mourning doves
I shall write my poems.

In dreams anyway,
I can at least fulfill her wish:
I lean to my love
as he dozes beside me
and whisper the words of her song.

In utter silence,
asking nothing in return,
with barely a bow,
they part on the sixth of the month,
two women and their man.

One autumn ago
three of us came to feed nuts
to carp in this pond.
Now cold morning breezes find
just two of us hand in hand.

It was only
the thin thread of a cloud,
almost transparent,
leading me along the way
like an ancient sacred song.

Were they bitter or
were they somehow sweet, the tears
that youthful priest shed
there on the street when he
first looked at me?

With the young monk
dozing beside the window
that crisp spring morning,
I caught my kimono sleeve
on a large stack of sutras.

After two long months
lodged in this Kyoto inn,
I've done nothing but
write poems. O Kamo River
plovers, I no longer love!

On her cheek and mine,
although our minds so differ,
like utter strangers,
the pine winds blow equally—
almost as though we were friends.

Picking wild roses,
some to weave into my hair
and some for the hand,
I then waited for hours,
I waited for you all day.

Late last autumn
it was she who leaned
against this old post
remembering plum blossoms
in your parting poem.

After twenty years
of living the barren life,
I want to believe
that now all my patient dreams
will at last be realized.

Twenty years of
living the desperate life
ring clearly, he cried
that day in Osaka,
reciting my bitter poems.

Before your leaving,
we paused on that dark evening
to write on a post
a poem about the white
flower of bush clover.

Lifting your head,
my slender arm beneath
the nape of your neck,
I want, suddenly, to suck
your feverish lips with mine.

Rather than trying
to touch the burning passion
pulsing beneath my soft
pale skin, you preach morality.
Aren't you awfully lonely?

The little lamb's eyes,
desperate for forest water,
must resemble mine.
O you whose love I long for,
how can you understand me?

Feeling you nearby,
how could I not come
to walk beneath
this evening moon rising
over flowering fields.

All day yesterday
I questioned the outcome
of desperate love.
Even then I cried as hope
gave way to loneliness.

Is it anyone's fault
that I who was once innocent
as the whitest silk
in constellations of stars
would fall into this world?

If I could, I would
put poisonous honey
on the burning lips
of all the desperate young
who are searching long for love.

What can I put in
my burning mouth now the blood
from my lover's finger—
he asked me to kiss it—
begins to dry on my lips.

O my beloved god
of the long night, you say,
"I must go. Farewell."
And your hem brushes by me.
And tears dampen my long hair.

Please forgive me.
I am not allowed to live
in this world. Saké,
pale lavender, just sends me
and I'm hopelessly lost.

Yesterday you spoke
of your love life's history.
Alone and sleepless,
twisting, my jealousy burns
through the merciless night.

Concentrated so
completely on each other
I can't tell us apart:
you, the white bush clover,
from me, the soft white lily.

Clinging to a Bible,
I knelt before my lover's
parents' tomb. At dusk,
I cried out, "Miroku!"—
name of the Future Buddha.

Camellias and
plum blossoms are equally white.
But pink peach blossoms
don't amplify the shame
heaped upon my many sins.

Agreed, we have
no talent for poetry.
We smile. This love
will last twenty thousand years.
Is that a long time or brief?

At my lover's
parents' grave, the pure white plum
is immaculate
beside the striped bamboo grass
in slowly falling twilight.

Kyoto, autumn,
peering deeply into water,
she bit her finger.
The falling drops of blood
make me want to shudder.

Wakening me
humming our favorite song,
he hands me a comb
and suggests I tidy my hair.
Embarrassed, I blush with shame.

Friends, please don't ask
whatever remains of love.
And don't preach to me.
Let our poetry endure.
It is the cross we bear.

My shiny black hair
fallen into disarray,
a thousand tangles,
like a thousand tangled thoughts
about my love for you.

Almost transparent
white and soft, my kimono
makes me despise
this faintly flickering
late night candlelight.

A huge array
of brilliantly colored
spring flowers line
the casket of
my beautiful friend.

He stood by the door,
calling through the evening
the name of my
sister who died last year
and how I pitied him!

Even at nineteen,
I had come to realize
that violets fade,
spring waters soon run dry,
this life too is transient.

All the red and white
peonies have fallen
and lie trampled.
Among the five Zen temples,
only these endless disputes.

Lingering with him
along the inn's balcony,
watching the river,
my long kimono sleeves
as long as my bottomless grief.

Spring quickly passes.
All the things of this world are
temporal! I cried,—
And lifted his hand to touch
my trembling, waiting breast.

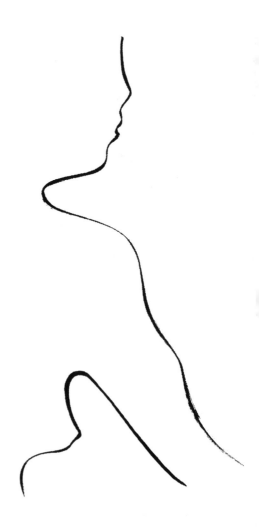

The blossoming plum
bright pink in the morning mist
above this valley—
these mountains are beautiful,
and I am beautiful too.

To paint my soft lips
bright crimson, I must make do
with my writing brush,
its tip almost frozen
in the cold morning dawn.

Who might that be,
giving voice to all the
lonely sorrows of
her life where bellflowers bloom
behind the monastery?

Both he and I
were just barely nineteen
when we saw our faces
reflected in the waters
of this gently flowing stream.

Was it a thousand
years ago or only
yesterday we parted?
Even now, on my shoulder,
I feel your friendly hand.

The evening dark
with dense fog and the candle
guttering out—how
fortuitous! He was so
very beautiful that night!

The river of stars
begins to part high
in the Milky Way while
through the curtains of our bed
I lie awake and watch.

In return for all
the sins and crimes of men,
the gods created me
with glistening long black hair
and pale, inviting skin.

Ignoring the ways
of right or wrong, eternal
life or lasting fame,
we turn to face each other,
loved and lover, face to face.

Modern-Style Poems

Mountain Moving Day

"Mountain moving day has come,"
is what I say. But no one believes it.
Mountains were just sleeping for a while.
Earlier, they had moved, burning with fire.
But you do not have to believe it.
O people! You'd better believe it!
All the sleeping women move
now that they awaken.

The Only Question

This one thing
I will ask you:
are you with the people
or apart from them?
Depending on your answer,
you and I
will be forever divided
between earth and heaven.

A Wish about Poetry

Poetry is the sculpture of real feelings.
There is a shadow between line and line
and between stanza and stanza,
a shadow that envelops details
is depth;
in proportion to its depth
let bits of natural flesh
rise to float clearly
on the surface of the lines.

My poetry is clay-work.
The sculpture of real feelings
does not depend upon materials.
Omit, omit!
I would not add anything extra,
even a line.
Let bits of natural flesh
rise to float clearly
on the surface of the lines.

The Universe and Myself

Born from the universe
and now in the universe,
somehow I'm away from the universe.
Therefore, I am lonely.
I am lonely even if I am with you,
but sometimes
I return again to the universe.
I do not know whether I am the universe
or the universe is myself.
At that time my heart is the heart of the universe;
at that time my eyes are the eyes of the universe;
at that time when I cry,
I cry, forgetting everything.
Surely it rains.
But I am lonely today.
I am away from the universe.
I am lonely even if I am with you.

Self-Awareness

From the day when, after saying inadvertently,
"I have decided to die,"
I saw a shaking man, surprised and pale,
my desire to die completely disappeared.
To tell you the truth, from that day
I came to know my world.

Women Are Plunder

Huge department store sales
seduce women's hearts
more than festivals or celebrations.
Some women, all their lives, find no attraction in the
    opposite sex.
Some women don't want to give birth to children.
Some women do not enjoy plays, music,
tea, novels, or poetry.
But hearing of big sales at Mitsukoshi and Shirokiya,
where is the woman
who won't get excited?
Wouldn't she become megalomaniacal . . . ?
At that instant all women
(even the class of women who spend half a day
hesitating
before buying even half a roll of muslin)
become emotional aristocrats,
peacocks among people.
I like this joviality.
Although I abandoned God early on,
I am humble before beauty:
an eternal believer.

But recently
I have been feeling terrible anxiety
and deep dread.
My excitement vanishes,
my frantic fever quickly cools.
Then I would certainly say,
"What a stupid African king I am!"
I would scold myself
and blush,
then suffer horrible pangs of conscience.

Among women who stride through the thresholds
    of huge
department stores?
Are there any who are not plunder?
Plunder: the very word is scary.
But there are so many women in the world
leading lives deserving of this word
and who are not ashamed!
Women rob men of their financial power
as if it were their own,
from father, older brother, younger brother,
    husband,
all men who earn knowledge, passion, blood and
    sweat,
the result of labor.

Even money for buying cheap lining for a collar
does not belong to women.
Women exploit men
for all the incredible money
that must be paid
to clothing shops, cosmetic shops, and jewelry shops.
Women!
(Among them, me.)
For what reason on earth are you
who are ignorant, incapable, and unreflective
    receiving
such inconceivable rewards from men?
If you haven't refined love and wise thoughts
to match your gorgeous clothes,
how can you maidens possibly be respected
by young men anywhere in the world?
As wives,
how fully have you understood your husbands' work
and helped?
As the better half of your husband,
which problems can you discuss as an equal?
Have you by your own labors earned
money for even one day's food?
As mothers,
what have you taught your own children?
Have you ever inspired your children

with vast spiritual dimensions
that no one else could open?
First, do you understand the responsibilities of
    motherhood?

Oh, I think of this
and I shudder.
How hateful, cursed, pitiful,
and shameful women are—I am, myself.
Women are plunder, for their laziness
and dependency,
stealing power from fathers, brothers, and husbands,
even eating the flesh of their own children.

I like the jubilant atmosphere
inside Mitsukoshi and Shirokiya.
I want to love the God of Beauty
without anxiety and fear,
but that requires courage.
First I must free myself of parasitic dependency
    on men,
and purify my soul and hands
with my own blood.
First I will work.
I will betray all women.
I will remove myself from the word *plunder.*

All women, myself,
how do you contribute to the culture
of village, city, or country?
Obeying signs in big department stores,
you try to decorate your small pale bodies
as the best and noblest,
the prized,
as if you are privileged.
Oh, what incredible tolerance from men!
Oh, what inconceivable arrogance!

The Town of Amazement

Arriving at a distant place,
I'm looking now at a very strange town,
a weird town without soldiers,
without a neighboring country to provide a
     convenient war.
University professors moonlight as firemen.
Doctors don't charge for medicine,
rather, depending upon the disease,
they hand out national bank notes
for the cost of convalescence.
No reporters investigate sinister accidents,
because there are no sinister accidents.
There are ministers but no ministries.
Ministers go to the fields,
work in factories
and pastures,
write novels, paint pictures.
Some even drive carts and clean the street.
Women never overdress.
They keep their beauty, are quiet, pure,
and never gossip.
They neither complain nor indulge conceit.
They hold down jobs the same as men.

Judges are especially honorable when they are
    women.
Courts, of course, don't deal with civil or criminal
    affairs,
but issue awards and citations.
When necessary, critics become lawyers,
they don't engage in long useless speeches.
They are usually quiet.
If they speak at all, they are terse
because distinguished people receiving awards make
    honest confessions,
and at the same time, the women who judge them
    are wise.
And this town doesn't have loan sharks,
no temples, no churches.
There are no detectives.
There are fewer than ten kinds of magazines.
There are no student plays.
And yet cabinet meetings,
wedding ceremonies, funerals,
literary gatherings, painters' meetings,
educational conferences, Diet sessions,
musical concerts, dance recitals.
Of course, plays with famous stars
are held at the largest national theaters.
It is indeed a strange town.

It is so different from
my beloved Tokyo.
Coming from such a distant place,
I am now looking at a very strange town.

Cold Supper

Oh, what will become of us
now that effort and wisdom are exhausted?
The fact that we cannot obtain
even a little money
is the reason we must suffer.
Unable to garner what little I'm rightly entitled to
because of slumping sales at bookstores,
for months we've lived by a painful budget,
forced to bow our heads and borrow.
Oh, and now we arrive at this dead end.

Seeing us superficially,
people would say we do not live within our means.
Of course that must be true.
But how could we possibly
labor more dutifully?
Isn't this a dreadful disaster,
enduring long labors
for so little in return?
Can we help our family, at least,
avoid this fate?

Of course we didn't pay rent today.
And all the bills of two or three months pile up
with our feelings of obligation.
Once our excuses
were only excuses,
but now they are unwilling lies.
Today I told a lie
knowing it was a lie.
How could I tell the truth?

Our innocent children
celebrated the Emperor's birthday today.
Hikaru is excited
about his own birthday tomorrow,
and his brothers and sisters
are as joyful as in all the years before.
Oh, we two, parents, ate a cold supper
watching the fresh young faces
of all the children
at the four sides of two low tables.

At last we will fall overboard,
we will reveal our concealed lies.
We will not be able to keep up appearances.
More than ten members of our family will actually
    starve.

This is certain:
here comes the day when we must restore ourselves.
This is the day in the midst of ice
when we, naked and cold,
must test ourselves by barely
touching shame, insanity, and suicide.

You Shall Not Be Killed, Brother!

Lamenting my younger brother Soshichi
in the besieging army at Port Arthur.

O my dear brother, I am in tears for you:
you should not be killed.
You were the last-born,
most adored by your parents.
Did your parents teach you to wield the sword to
    murder other people?
Did your parents raise you
for twenty-four years
to kill and to die?

Since you inherit your parents' name
as proud master of our renowned shop
in Sakaishi,
you should not be killed.
Even if Port Arthur's castle falls,
so what?
You are not aware that killing is not in harmony
with the customs of a merchant family.

You should not be killed.
The Honorable Emperor would not personally

engage in the war.
Since the Emperor's heart is so merciful,
how could he possibly ask
others to shed blood
and die like beasts
and believe that dying is honor?

O my brother,
you should not be killed in battle!
It's said this era is peaceful,
but our mother protects the family
in great sorrow from the death of our father
and now, pained
by her child's conscription,
her hair grows ever whiter.

Have you forgotten your new young wife
lying delicate and beautiful in tears behind her
    curtain?
Do you still think of her?
Separated after barely ten months wedded,
think of her virginal heart.
Since you are the only you in the world,
whom can she rely on?
You should not be killed, my brother!

Love

The emotional duration of ancient love,
endlessly, day after day,
talking to each other constantly.

How intense love is now.
As we usually pretend we don't really know each
    other,
our hearts suddenly become tense,
leaving us helpless with love
just like burning magnesium,
just like steam from a leaking locomotive,
just like the dying swan,
screaming and writhing in its body.

First Labor Pains

I am feeling bad today.
My body is feeling bad.
I am lying in bed before childbirth,
silent, with my eyes open.

Despite frequent brushes with death
and having gotten used to pain, blood, and screams,
why am I trembling with uncontrollable
anxiety and fear?

A young doctor consoled me and
told me about the happiness of birth.
I know it much better than he.
How useful is that now?

Knowledge does not belong to reality.
Experience belongs to the past.
Please, everyone, be quiet!
Would you remain as observers?

I am simply alone.
I am simply alone in heaven and on earth.
I will wait for my own act of God,
quietly biting my lip.

To give birth
is the only creation of truth
which actually explodes from within me.
There is no room for good and evil.

Now, the first labor pains . . .
The sun suddenly grows pale,
the world coldly calms down
and I am simply alone . . .

A Blow from My Son August

O my dear two-year-old August,
I am writing this for you.
Today for the first time,
you struck your mother's cheek.
Your self-discovering power!
The pure conquering power
of your young life
expressed in anger
and a convulsive fit
blazed like an electric fire!
You were probably unaware of anything.
And you must have soon forgotten.
But I—your mother—was astonished
and was truly happy.
Someday, as a man,
you will courageously stand on your own feet
and stand virtuously like a man
and will love people and nature beyond limit
(the center of conquest is love)
and will overcome
suspicion, suffering, jealousy and death,
dirty tricks, insult and tyranny, academic
    opportunism,

conventionalism, ambitions of the nouveau riche,
    mere status.
That's it! That authentic blow
is actually your whole life!
With the pain of sharp blows
from your lion cub palm,
I was happy to have
a golden premonition,
and suddenly feel our common power
lurking within myself,
the cheek you struck
so that even the cheek you didn't hit grew fevered.
You were probably unaware.
You probably soon forgot.
But when you become an adult,
when you think and when you work
and when you fall in love and when you fight,
take this poem and read it,
my dear two-year-old August:
I am writing this for you.
Today, for the first time,
you struck your mother's cheek.

O August, ever more dear to me,
you in Mother's womb
were touring Europe.

As you mature,
your wisdom will recall
the memory of that journey—
what Michelangelo, Rodin,
Napoleon, and Pasteur did
is it!—your authentic blow,
that blow of ferocious ecstasy.

Index of First Lines

About the Translators and the Artist

SAM HAMILL is the author of over thirty books of poetry, translations, and essays, including *The Erotic Spirit: An Anthology of Poems and Sensuality, Love, and Longing.* He has been the recipient of fellowships from the National Endowment of the Arts, the Guggenheim Foundation, the U.S.-Japan Friendship Commission, and Lila Wallace-Reader's Digest Foundation.

KEIKO MATSUI GIBSON is a poet and translator who teaches literature at Kanda University in Chiba, Japan. She is the author of *Stir Up the Perceptible World,* a bilingual collection of her poetry.

STEPHEN ADDISS is a professor of art and humanities at the University of Richmond. The author of several books on Zen art and culture, his calligraphy and paintings have been exhibited internationally.

Shambhala Centaur Editions

After Ikkyu and Other Poems
by Jim Harrison

The Book of the Heart: Embracing the Tao
by Loy Ching-Yuen
Translated by Trevor Carolan and Bella Chen

Dewdrops on a Lotus Leaf: Zen Poems of Ryokan
Translated by John Stevens

Four Huts: Asian Writings on the Simple Life
Translated by Burton Watson

Look! This Is Love: Poems of Rumi
Translated by Annemarie Schimmel

Midnight Flute: Chinese Poems of Love and Longing
Translated by Sam Hamill

Only Companion: Japanese Poems of Love and Longing
Revised and Expanded Edition
translated by Sam Hamill

Prayer of the Heart: Writings from the *Philokalia*
Compiled by Saint Nikodimos of the Holy Mountain
and Saint Makarios of Corinth
Translated by G. E. H. Palmer, Philip Sherrard, and Kallistos Ware

Songs of the Sons and Daughters of Buddha
Translated by Andrew Schelling and Anne Waldman

A Touch of Grace: Songs of Kabir
Translated by Linda Hess and Shukdev Singh

Wild Ways: The Zen Poems of Ikkyu
Translated by John Stevens

Printed in the United States
by Baker & Taylor Publisher Services